DREAMS

Principles to Live What You Love!

DAYO OLATOKUN

Published and distributed in the United States by Dayo Olatokun, Far Rockaway, New York

Copyright © 2021 by Dayo Olatokun All rights reserved. No parts of this book may be reproduced by any mechanical, photographic, or electronic process, or in the form of phonographic recording; nor may it be stored in a retrieval system, transmitted, or otherwise be copied for public or private use – other than for "fair use" as brief quotations embodied in articles and reviews – without prior written permission of the publisher.

The author intends to offer information of a general nature to help you in your quest to advocate for your life's goals, dreams, aspirations, and well-being. In the event you use any of the information in this book for yourself, which is your constitutional right, the author or publisher assume no responsibility for your actions.

Scriptures quoted from www.biblegateway.com

Book Coach – Pen Publish Profit, LLC
Cover Design – Okomota
Editing – Robin Devonish
Interior Design – Istvan Szabo, Ifj.
Photographer – Ted Ely
ISBN: 978-1-7359712-1-6

ACKNOWLEDGMENTS

Thank you for the brotherhood I have with each of you individually to my brothers from another mother, Moses, Larry, and Reese. We've seen each other through the worst, so cheers to the best that's yet to come!

Special thank you to my professors from the hard knocks school: Pastor Adrian & LaDedra Ewings; you have served as my bachelor's program. Dr. Jonathan & Sabrina Shaw, you have served as my master's program. Your influence on faith, family, and leadership is embedded in my core as a man. Thank you all for looking out for me.

To my parents, Timothy & Yemisi Olatokun, thank you for giving me life. Your love and discipline have helped shape the way I see the world. I always tell people, "The belt saved my life." Thank you! I hope to continually make you proud and take care of you the way you have taken care of us!

To my siblings: Michael, Mary, and Gabriel Olatokun. We all we got! God knows we have been through so much, yet we are stronger than ever. I'm proud of each of you and can't wait to celebrate the many accomplishments you'll achieve on your journeys!

"In order for black lives to matter. Africa must matter" - Burna Boy.

I am eternally grateful to be African. Cheers to all my fellow Nigerians living and pursuing their Pipe Dreams. AWA NI YEN!

Thank you, my first manager Jenn Lederer for seeing that I had more to offer than just acting. You encouraged me to purchase my domain name dayoolatokun.com and now I am finally using it to be the inspiration that you saw.

Thank you, Robin Devonish, for the encouragement to start this project and all your publishing expertise throughout the journey. Also, for watching your goddaughters every time I needed you. You are clutch!

My company, G.P.A., has grown tremendously over the years, and it would not have been possible without two incredibly special board members and friends. Roosevelt Smith and Tyisha Williams, thank you for your endless contributions and support of this vision!

I love you all dearly and super grateful for your prayers and support of my Crown Ministries family!

The 619, you will always hold a special place in my heart! To all my GODSENT friends in San Diego who loved and supported me during my starving artist days...You know who you are...thank you!

To my guys in Florida: Trevor, Shawn, Willey, Amos, and Ernest. O-town was the first stop on my PIPE Dreams journey right out of high school. You brothers accepted me and my colorful personality with laughter and love. Cheers to more laughs because we are crazy!

Special thank you to QIRT! Mr. Staley, thank you for the opportunity to bring G.P.A. to your campus. I am forever grateful for you signing off on this partnership! Ms. Larcher and Ms. Edmund, thank you for welcoming me with open arms and sharing your beloved classrooms. You are phenomenal teachers and amazing human beings! Thank you, Mr. Manalo (Former Principal), Mr. Singh (current principal), faculty, staff, and of course, EVERY QIRT STUDENT I've had the pleasure of pouring into! I look forward to our continued partnership.

Thank you to Nicole Hamilton from GGE for allowing me to introduce G.P.A. to your program. It was still in the developmental stages, and you gave me the room to develop! To my colleagues during my GGE days: Marguerite Copeland, Shaheed K. Woods, and Asha John...thank you!

Thank you to Big Du from Ocean Village, who introduced me to Denean Ferguson, who connected me to Jaqueline

Gutierrez at P.S./M.S. 43, where I held the very first GPA workshop in the spring of 2015! Mrs. Ferguson, you are forever the Mayor of Far Rockaway.

I send much love to my hometown Far Rockaway, a.k.a. The 53rd State and the 6th Borough. We are ONE PENINSULA!

I DEDICATE THIS BOOK TO...

My children, Destini, Hope, and Jae'Shaun. My Pipe Dreams will always live with you as my legacy. You are all uniquely gifted and admirably compassionate. If you live the life you were created to live, nothing is impossible for you!

To my Queen, honey, right hand, and wife, Beans (insider) Dawn, you are the epitome of support! Years ago, when we were dating, you told me I would write a book. I didn't believe you. Well, here it is! Thank you for all you do for our family and for always having my back. I love you to the end.

FOREWORD

There is an old statement that says a man's purpose is hidden in his daily routine. You can discover your reason for existence within your daily activities and assignments. The things you do every day will predict how your tomorrow will look and what you will eventually become.

The challenge with this is that most people aren't intrinsically aware of their life. Most people do not base their life on a set of principles and core values that will ground them in their decisions and position them for their future. Principles and core values are the platforms and stages that your life dreams stand upon. Without a sufficient value system, you will not discover your passion and be blinded to your life's calling.

Principles or core values are fundamental beliefs that you obtain through life experiences, and they help shape who you are as a person or an organization. Every major organization and successful person have a set of core values and principles that they live and exist by. Whether it is a multi-billion-dollar organization or a prominent actor or executive, they each possess an internal set of rules that guides them in their daily decision-making process. No matter what happens or who comes or goes, these rules will determine how they will govern themselves and move forward. That's just the thing with core values – they don't change easily. That's why one must think long and hard before establishing what principles they will live by. No matter the changes of trends, economy, politics, or powers, your core values will remain the same, and they guide you on what you should do next or how you should handle certain matters.

One major thing that one must discover to actualize core values is to find out what your purpose is in life. Your purpose for existing will point directly to what your value system is. A street pharmaceutical specialist (drug dealer) has a different value system than a mechanical engineer. Now, I don't argue that a person's purpose is to be an illegal drug pusher, but too many people assume that is the only option they have. But whatever someone perceives their purpose to be, that purpose shapes the values.

You may ask, how does one discover their purpose? Well, it's quite simple. Answering these three simple questions can help you in discovering what purpose.

1. What do you love doing even if you weren't paid to do it?
2. What do you hate to see in our society?
3. What would you decide to do today if money wasn't an option?

Answering these three questions will point directly to your purpose. When you assess your love for something, express hatred of another, and pursue a dream without the hindrance of finances, your purpose is standing right there. That thing is the reason for your existence. When you begin to pursue it, you will find your passions awakening. You will discover your drive in life, and the energy you thought died will arise in you. Now, this process may take some time, but if it is a pursuit of yours, you are on the right path. After discovering your purpose, those core values will begin to take shape, and you'll be on your way to living a fulfilled life of success and accomplishments.

As you read this phenomenal book written by a phenomenal man, my hope and prayer are that you will develop principles in life to live what you love. But don't be selfish; share this tool with everyone you know. The thing about a pipe dream is that there are many pipes and many dreams, but only one path for you. While someone may be on a different path, his or her dreams too can come to pass. In the words of the famous Brooklyn Rhythmic poet, "Biggie" – "*It was all a dream...*"

Dr. Jonathan I. Shaw, Sr.

CONTENTS

Intro 1
  The Sunday Night Struggle! 1
  95 Lexus 3
  Pipe Dreams 6

I. Punctuality 9
  You're Right On Time 9
  Be Where You Need To Be When You Need To Be There! 15
  Clear Intention 17
  Preparation 18
  Sacrifice 19

II. Integrity 27
  Decoded 27
  Climate Change 30
  Price Tag 32
  Mask On 33

III. Purpose 39
  Soul Power 39
  Choosy 44

Simmer 48
Forgive & Foreclose 50
Interest 53
Muse 58

IV. Excellence 67
Commitment 67
You Get What You Pay For 68
You Wanna Be Tired, Or You Wanna Win? 71
Allergic To Normal 74
Network 77

Outro 83
You Know Why I'm Here 83
Kill Or Be Killed 85
Rewrite History 87

INTRO

The Sunday Night Struggle!

I read a post on Instagram that said, "Monday's don't suck, your job does!" That statement struck a nerve because, like most working adults I know, I have little to no desire to return to work on Mondays once the weekend has concluded. This is a harsh reality! This post wouldn't have resonated with me back in high school or even college. However, as an adult with a family to feed, I understand the Sunday Night Struggle! It's that deep sigh that kicks in Sunday evenings, somewhere between 5 and 7 pm. We try to shift our minds back into gear for that Monday 'mourning' alarm clock, to the Monday 'mourning' commute, to the Monday 'mourning' clock- in, leading up to the infamous Monday 'mourning' phrase; I HATE THIS JOB!

'The Sunday Night Struggle' is an automated message recorded deep in our souls that says, "now back to our regularly scheduled program!"

The simple thought of going back to work on Mondays after a short weekend is disheartening to most working-class adults. However, the truth is there's nothing wrong with Mondays, the day itself. We know the day has been here long before we started working and will be around long after we retire...or die trying.

Mondays mean us no harm at all. It's that wretched, disrespectful, disloyal, unfulfilling, ungrateful, mentally, and emotionally draining J.O.B. that seems like a life sentence to the average working-class citizen.

Fortunately, there is a different perspective on Mondays that we can glean from. A small fraction of people on this earth actually love what they do. Or as I'd like to say, LIVE WHAT THEY LOVE! These are the "weirdos" who love Mondays. In an interview, Writer/Comedian Marlon Wayans stated how he hates the weekends because he must break from doing what he loves. He looks forward to Mondays because he can go back to work! Work for him is writing, directing, producing, and overall being creative! Notice I didn't say he gets to go back to his job...NO. He gets to go back to work! There is a difference between the two. Your job is what someone pays you to do, which fulfills their vision and barely meets your needs to survive. Your work is what you were born to do AND get paid for it. Successful people who are fulfilled look forward to Mondays because they get to go back to using their gifts and talents, earning a living doing what they love!

Pursuing a career in doing what you love doesn't require in-depth scientific research. It requires deep self-reflection. It's important to discover where we're gifted. Self-discovery is a journey towards fulfillment. To discover the area(s) where we're gifted, we must go back to the time when we weren't inundated with bills, dependents, and responsibilities. Here are some questions to ask yourself on this road to self-discovery.

1. What did you do for fun?
2. What were you extremely good at and was known for during the years of adolescence and young adulthood?
3. What did you habitually practice during those years that very few, if anyone, knows about, that provided an escape from your reality?

The answer to your question is likely where you're gifted! Whether it is singing in the shower, being the class clown, or drawing while the teacher is giving a lecture, your gift is the natural ability you've had since you were a kid! From entertainment to administration, everyone has gifts and talents that people would pay good money for. The problem is those gifts were not identified and developed during the days of our youth. As a result, we have this great disdain for a day we were meant to look forward to - Mondays!

What am I saying? If you're anything like me who has a dream and a job competing for your sanity, this book is for you!

<u>95 Lexus</u>

One night at bedtime, under my comforter, with the AC blasting, listening to 90's R&B, in the back of my 1995 Lexus, parked in the fancy Sherman Oaks section of Los Angeles, I had a life-changing revelation and preview of a program I'd start several years later. I saw myself back in New York, helping young people in my Far Rockaway community discover their talents early so they wouldn't have to struggle like me to fulfill their pipe dreams. I had no idea what to do with the vision at the time. I didn't know where to start or even the clarity of what this vision was in totality. I had enough on my plate using my 24-hour fitness membership as a place to shower every morning. I just knew I didn't want the generation behind me to repeat this glorified "starving artist" life. It only looks good on TV because there's usually a triumphant ending we get to see! All I know is I went to sleep that night with the thought of helping youth, especially the creative ones, avoid the starving artist's path to success.

After four years of living in Cali to pursue an acting career that didn't quite pan out as expected, I moved back home to NYC. Hopefully, the home-court advantage would get me closer to my pipe dream of becoming an actor. I applied to NYU before coming home and was accepted soon after I arrived. The plan was to finish my degree in theater and work in the industry that way. Unfortunately, my financial aid and scholarships weren't enough to cover the lifestyles of the rich and famous sized tuition. ("Lifestyles of the rich and famous" is a pop song from the early 2000s by a group named Good Charlotte). In addition to that, I could not get a cosigner for a student loan to cover the balance. Therefore, I surrendered my admission. From that point, my life consisted of auditions and odd jobs to make money.

One day, around 2014, I was going to the store and ran into a friend of mine who was furious with her son. She came to me and said, "Dayo talk to this boy before I kill him!" When I asked what he did, she said, "He's always breaking stuff in my house!" I told her I'd talk to him. When I saw him, I went off! "What's your problem? Why are you breaking stuff in your mother's house? Who do you think you are?" I mean, I came for his life! He replied, "Yo, Dayo, chill, chill, it's not even like that." I said, "So tell me what it's like!" He then gave me a response that came with the revelation that helped kick start my company. He said, "Dayo, I break stuff in the house so I can put it together!" In other words, he thrived off building, constructing, designing, etc. He would take a table apart piece by piece to become familiar with the parts and put it back together. At that moment, I didn't see the savage he was portrayed to be. I saw an engineer, an architect, a construction worker, and an interior designer all at once! What mom perceived as a problem was simply the boy's process of engagement and fulfillment.

At ten years old, it was evident where he was gifted, at least in one area. What he needed was the proper education and training to make this perceived hobby an actual profession. Therefore, his middle school should have a strong STEM component, as should his high school. I shared that his college or trade school major should be in construction management, architecture, design, engineering, or something in that arena. By the time he begins filling out college applications, he would already have an eight-year portfolio full of STEM-related projects and experience, making him more attractive for universities and trade schools, leading to SCHOLARSHIPS! Rather than hoping he gets accepted to a school, he can have options from who's offering the most money for him to be trained and certified!

This moment is where GPA was developed in my mind. GPA is the acronym for The Gifted & Purposed Alliance, Inc. This is my arts-based youth development program that helps young people identify their gifts and talents, so they can ultimately earn a living doing what they love! Who knew that night in my 95 Lexus was a revelation to a non-profit I would create three years later?

Pipe Dreams

Write five things you love to do that may be considered a "Pipe Dream."

1 _____

2 _____

3 _____

4 _____

5 _____

One or more of these passion points will become the Mondays you look forward to after reading this book. What is a "pipe dream?" It's a term used when people say your chances of fulfilling that burning desire are slim to none, one in a million, or outright impossible.

One of the responses I received when I first told family and friends I wanted to be an actor was, "finish college, then get a real job. Hollywood is just a pipe dream." What may seem like a pipe dream to others could be a reality for you if you're willing to drown out the noise of their disbelief. Like Lupita Nyongo said when receiving her Oscar for 12 Years A Slave: "Your dreams are valid!"

To achieve any dream, particularly the ones considered "pipe dreams," you need some principles to stand on. The four principles to **P.I.P.E** are **Punctuality, Integrity, Purpose, and Excellence!** If you adopt them, you will be able to create a pipeline to those dreams. But before we get there, let's focus on the word 'Pipe' for a minute. Every building or house that functions or is deemed livable has pipes within its walls. Inside those pipes is an element we all need, its called water. To gain access to the water, whether to drink or wash, you wouldn't break the walls open to bust the pipes and gain access to the water. The proper action would be to turn a knob to open the faucet. This way the water can flow and be used to meet your needs. With this illustration, metaphorically speaking, you do have pipe dreams. Within you resides gifts, talents, abilities, and values that no one sees, but they exist. People can see the walls you put up to protect yourself but may not see the gifts flowing inside you. That's why to them; it's just a pipe dream. They can't see it! But it's there. Not only is it there, but precious once it's released. Just open the faucet so your gifts can begin to flow where there's a demand for them. You are too valuable to hide behind the walls you put up. You have what someone needs to survive, and these principles will be your pipeline! The first principle is *punctuality*. We begin with punctuality because no matter how gifted you are, you must navigate working on someone else's time until you're in the position to set your own schedule!

I. PUNCTUALITY

I see punctuality from two perspectives, first, generally understanding the importance of being on time for the agenda, and second, the power of timing: the impact of WHEN something happens.

<u>You're Right On Time</u>

You did not get to choose where you were born, by whom you were born, or even what period you were born into. However, you do have the right to your perspective of your era's struggles. You also can make an impact through your gift(s). The period you were born into presents challenges your gifts have the power to speak to. Your gift(s) can put your perspective on a platform.

When Sam Cooke wrote the hit song "A Change Is Gonna Come," he was not an elected official or a famous civil rights activist. He was simply an artist who had a perspective of his era's conditions based on his experience. He then put that perspective on his gifted platform, which gave hope to our ancestors during the fight for civil rights. The timing of this song is what I want to highlight. Not only did it speak to our ancestors' struggle and provide them an encouraging thought to hold on to, but it's become a mantra of every black empowerment movement from the civil rights era to our present-day Black Lives Matter movement.

When you use your gift(s) to speak to your generation's challenges, you give your perspective a platform, which has the potential to make an impact that transcends time and traditions. From Sam Cooke's inspirational hymn to Muhammad Ali's stance against the Vietnam War to Colin Kaepernick taking a knee against the national anthem, the timing in which they used their gifts put their perspective on a platform that left a massive impact. They will be referenced for many generations to come!

YOU have the capacity for transcendent impact based on how quickly you grasp this concept of timing and consciousness within your era. Your impact can be global or local, depending on which industry places a demand on your gift(s). A famous athlete and a passionate social worker can both have an incredible impact. The difference is in the size of their audience. I believe we can identify our audience during the years of our youth. However, based upon the communities some of us have been forced to grow up in, it's improbable. There is no more incredible pool of talent in the world than the hood, inner-city, or whatever term you're familiar with. If you're reading this and have only heard of "the hood" or you've only seen it on TV, let me give you the dummy dissertation of what it is.

The hood can be any housing project, housing complex, or poverty-stricken area where people of color make up most of the population as residents and claim that area with pride.

The hood is composed of numerous people within a 3-10 block radius or more, depending on the city. Within that radius are some of the most gifted, talented, and creative human beings on this planet! We have some of the world's greatest writers, speakers, thinkers, inventors, athletes, and artists this world will NEVER see. Regrettably, many will never come close to using those talents because they remain focused on survival. It's challenging to pursue a prosperous future when your past is built on survival. However, there are always people from every hood, fortunately, who experience the miracle of exposure. The exposure simultaneously gives a future to run towards and a past to run from. Every time you're exposed to an experience outside of your norm, there's a potential for you to realize where you're gifted and become obsessed with your creativity. This can lead you to form lasting relationships with the right people and ultimately claw your way out of the hood motivated by a pipe dream.

The concept of timing develops each byproduct of exposure.

Again, you have zero control over when and where you were born, but you have the capacity for impact during that time. Take a good look at where you are in life right now. Whether you're in grade school, higher education (college, trade school, vocational school, etc.), or working a 9-5. What impact have you had on your era? When your name is mentioned, what can people attach it to? You shouldn't be burdened by what you do throughout the entire course of your life. What you've done in the past is already done and can't be reversed. What lies ahead is a legacy that's still being captured in frames. You'll either be praised or criticized for the impact you make in small frames of time.

We can make an impact in every frame of our lives. Think about it: There's a memory people have of us in elementary school, there's a thought or theme we're associated with from middle school, and of course, the greatest social hub of our youth, high school! Each of these frames consists of memories we've created based upon the impact we've had, whether they're perceived as major or minor. The 'Impact' is not what YOU remember, but rather HOW you're remembered!

To my young people reading this, it may seem like grade school is a difficult place to measure impact. If you look closer, this is a period of your life where your schedule is set for you. All you have to do is show up and do your best in the classes you were assigned. Of course, you will love some classes more than the others, it's natural. Every subject isn't for everybody. Loving them or not speaks to your interests. The most effective way to have an impact is to gravitate towards your interests. Both your academic and social interests will allow you to be YOU in your purest form. The best educators have the foresight to help navigate these interests.

To my educators reading this, you must recognize perceived negative behavior, which can positively impact the entire student body. You can help them navigate where that interest or behavior could be of great use. We know hindsight is 2020, but yearbooks are clear indicators of a student's interest if they were magically available for every incoming freshman. "Class clowns" who give you a hard time and are suspended continuously may benefit from joining the drama club or host a student lead TV/radio show. The student who was voted "Most likely to succeed" could be asked to help tutor the "Best Athlete" that's always asleep in class. What about the disrespectful and noticeably disinterested student because the school doesn't offer any financial literacy course, sports management/medicine program, or anything that serves his/her interests besides the school team? The tutor can develop peer mentorship skills, and the athlete can maintain a decent average because he/she might be more receptive to feedback from their peers.

This foresight and navigation from educators and administration could help channel some of that perceived negative energy into constructive contributions, limiting the distractions during instructions because their served interests have incentivized them. But let's be real. Most of the schools in our districts are grossly underfunded, so there is no drama club, TV/radio studio, financial literacy, debate team, or cooking class. Many other beneficial enrichment programs that serve our young people's interest—leaving them to figure out how to obtain 44 credits and pass regents and state exams that do not translate to the work readiness skills they'll need to compete in their marketplace! As a result, the students who are not "Most likely to succeed" candidates develop ways to impact socially...which can often be at the wrong place and the wrong time.

So, to my young people, pay attention to the interests you have. That's the platform you have to impact every frame of your youth and adult life. If you're fortunate enough to attend a school that offers programs and courses that serve your interest, take the initiative, and sign up! Do not wait until high school or college. Timing is everything and your time is now!

To the students whose present school does not offer any programs or courses that serve your interests, start a petition to have a drama club, debate team, art studio, or whatever your interests are. Put pressure on your school to apply pressure on your district to fund these programs. That alone is impact within itself. At the same time, ask your parent/guardian to investigate local after school programs or community centers that may have them.

The bottom line is you want to develop your gift(s) as soon as you identify them so you can begin to produce what's already inside of you! Whatever frame of life you're currently in, you can impact that period. Whether you're in middle school, high school, higher education, or straight-up working, FOCUS ON YOUR FRAME! Don't be intimidated by the big picture of who you're "supposed" to be. When you focus your frame, the big picture will develop accordingly. Make an impact on your frame! The impact of recording artists is per album. Athletes are judged on production per season. Writers' impact is measured per book/essay/article/ script. Whatever you do will be praised or criticized based on what you produce during that time frame. Stop worrying about what other people think. No one cares about your future until you produce something in their presence they can't forget!

Legends are judged by what they accomplish during THEIR ERA. Whether you're a student or working adult, do not be intimidated by what others are accomplishing or how much time you think you've lost. Maximize this current frame of your life, and not only will you realize the impact you've already had, but the potential for transcending impact by tapping into your gift(s). If you start now, you're right on time!

<u>Be Where You Need To Be When You Need To Be There!</u>

When your physical presence is required at a pre-arranged time to fulfill a pre-arranged agenda, BE WHERE YOU NEED TO BE WHEN YOU NEED TO BE THERE!! Until you're in the position to create your schedule to generate income, you'll always be bound to the time someone created for you. This means there's always someone in charge you need to impress. For my adults, that would be the supervisor on your job. For my students, that would be the instructors in your classrooms. Your ability to show up on time significantly impacts how you are perceived by your superior(s).

Before you're graded on your work, you're judged on your time of arrival. Whether or not you successfully do the job, you can make a great impression by consistently being on time. A commitment to punctuality gives you a valuable lifeline every flawed human needs in times of trouble – THE BENEFIT OF THE DOUBT! If you ever find yourself on the brink of failure, whether at work or in school, your level of punctuality could potentially shift the decision or grade in your favor.

Aside from the benefit of the doubt from your superiors, punctuality puts you in a position to dominate your present status (school, job, etc.) to make strides toward your dreams and aspirations.

Let's be clear! This is all about YOUR PIPE Dreams—the big picture for YOUR life. Your big picture will never materialize if you're repeatedly hitting the snooze button! Your dreams will remain dreams until you wake up.

> *"The best way to make your dreams come true is to WAKE UP!"*
> ~ Paul Valery

Here are some punctuality tips I share in the GPA workshops with my students:

Clear Intention

Always keep your big picture in the forefront of your mind! When you have PIPE Dreams, you must both live in the future and function efficiently in the present. Anyone building a house needs to see the blueprint to keep in mind what the house WILL look like while constructing each phase precisely according to the plans.

Having a vision board helps keep your intentions clear and become faced with a daily reminder of why you get up and grind like you do. Consistently being on time for your present status builds the muscle memory you'll need to excel in your future endeavors.

Punctuality is a professional protocol required in any field you choose to earn a living from. But if you cannot master being on time on this level, you'll never make it to the level you see in your dreams. And if you do, you won't last very long. Because habits are built over time, use this frame of your life to develop this essential principle of punctuality! Treat your school, job, and important engagements like your PIPE dream when it comes to showing up on time. Give your present status your future effort! The reason you are fighting your way through this school, job, or status is because you want to ultimately LIVE WHAT YOU LOVE! Earn a living doing what you love.

You'll always have internal warfare when what you see doesn't match what you have. The lifestyle of your future rarely matches the resources of your present. However, your present possesses key contributors, such as, respect for time. For this reason, it is imperative to develop an inner discipline to remind yourself of the big picture. You don't have to show up on time to your job because you "love" your place of employment or your co-workers are the greatest! You don't make it on time to your first class EVERY DAY because you go to the BEST school in your district, or you have the GREATEST and FAIREST teachers your institution has to offer. Your commitment to *punctuality* is not based upon your love for where you currently are in life. You are *punctual* because you're obsessed with where you're trying to go!

> *"To be early is to be on time,*
> *to be on time is to be late,*
> *to be late is to be forgotten."*
> ~ Elin Hilderbrand

Preparation

I tell my students in every workshop that Sunday night is the key to the week. That should be the time you take out all your clothes for the week. Choose your outfits for Monday-Friday and iron everything Sunday night. Let's face it, some of us like to get fly, so we're not walking out of the house any old type of way. Therefore, having your clothes ready Sunday night can save you at least 20 minutes of prep time in the morning.

Do a read-through of all your due dates so it can sink into your system—everything from course assignments to extracurricular activities and even projects for work. A quick read through allows you to prioritize where your extra time should go for that week. This way, you can complete them in increments instead of trying to achieve this "huge task" at the last minute. Most of our assignments typically seem more strenuous than they should be, not because we're not smart enough or were given too much to do. The truth is we failed to adequately prepare or complete them on time. Anything done at the last minute will always feel like an unbearable burden. Some of you need to stop telling yourselves, "I work better under pressure." That is nothing but a front to cover up habits of irresponsibility. You may have gotten away with last-minute work in the past, but it's not always because you're good under pressure. The grace of God got you through. I'm telling you firsthand, grace can be exhausted!

Sacrifice

When I say something always comes up, I mean something ALWAYS comes up. It never fails! When you have a plan, a goal, an objective, something always pops up out of nowhere to slow you down or outright stop you from completing the task. Often, it's usually pretty important. It can be family-related or even something your heart can't stand to ignore. As of today, I need you to IGNORE it!

A few years ago, I had a call back for a role in a film I auditioned for. A call back means you made an impression in your initial audition that was good enough to be called back to read in front of the decision-makers.

I prepared better than I did the initial audition. I studied my lines more and had them committed to memory just as good as my own name. I believe my call back was at 10:00 am that date, so I checked the train schedule the night before and chose to take the train that would have me at the casting director's office by 9:15 am. I chose this time just in case there were any delays on the A train that day. We all know the MTA can be as unreliable as a dead beat on some days. Therefore, New Yorkers typically give a two-hour window for a commute, especially if you're from Far Rockaway. We struggle the most!

That morning I gave myself enough time to eat breakfast, go over my lines some more, and walk peacefully to the train station without rushing. On my way up the train station's stairs, I happened to look back and see a woman attempting to carry her toddler holding her hand and her infant in the stroller up the stairs. Of course, I chose to walk back down to help them up. My train was three minutes away, and I've helped women with strollers soooooo many times in the past, so I knew I had enough time to help them up and catch my train. Halfway up, she drops the baby bag. Unzipped, several items like bottles, toys, etc., within the bag, tumbled down the stairs. I continued to carry the stroller up by myself as she went down to pick up each item. The toddler then decides to chase the mother down the stairs, resulting in tripping and falling. Therefore, the mother turns back to pick up and console the crying child. I told her to come up the stairs to stand by the infant in the stroller, so I can go pick up the remaining items that fell. All of this happened within a matter of two minutes. Cognizant of the time, I ran down the stairs to pick up the remaining items. As I reached the bottom of the stairs, I heard the train coming. I ran up the stairs, gave the woman her items, then ran to the turnstile. I pulled out my wallet to get my metro card, and of course, I dropped it while rushing. My first swipe of the card was "too fast" for the turnstile read, of course, so I swiped again and took off running to the second flight of stairs. Before I reached the top, I heard the worst sound you could listen to when running for the train; "Stand clear of the closing doors, please!" I yelled, "hold the door, hold the door!" but no one held it. The door closed right in my face as I made it to the platform. You can only imagine how annoyed I was! However, I calmed down quickly because I knew the next train's schedule would allow me to arrive at the casting office by 9:40 am, still a fairly good time, right?

After sitting at the train station for 20 minutes, we get an announcement over the loudspeaker saying, "due to a police investigation at Mott Avenue (four stops away), trains are delayed. We apologize for any inconvenience." When I missed my train, I was annoyed. Now I was FURIOUS! In my head, I called that woman and her kids so many names too inappropriate for this book, so I'll just let you use your imagination. But at the end of the day, I had no one to blame but myself! I reached out to my agency to let them know the situation so they could inform the casting office. The train ultimately came, and I made it there around 10:30-ish. Fortunately, the casting office was understanding of the situation and allowed me to read for my part.

The moral of the story is I had no business going down to help that woman, given my train was only three minutes away. As much as helping people is a part of my nature, I should've just kept it moving. As mean as that may sound, the truth is the world typically doesn't care what your situation is and why you're late. I've been late to auditions in the past due to freeway traffic, accidents, or construction work (LA traffic is a different beast) and could not read my scene. If you can't be trusted to be on time for the audition, interview, or whatever the term is for your field, then they can't trust you to show up on time to work. You must make sacrifices to be on time. Something is always going to come up that's critical, and for the most part, could very well be important. However, it cannot take precedence over where you're trying to go.

When you commit to being punctual, people's priorities take a back seat to your purpose! Even if you're not where you want to be yet, you're building this habit along this journey for the big picture. And let me say this for those of you who are always burdened by family and close friends. You are NOT responsible for the irresponsibility of someone else! Everyone seems to come to YOU when they need assistance, caught up in a dilemma, or are habitually poor planners. And you're always there because you have a heart of gold. When you have somewhere to be, you need to sacrifice people's demands to be with your destiny! JUST SAY NO whenever you have to choose between people and purpose! Do not fear the "damage" your rare no may do to a relationship. If your no is all it takes to strain any relationship, then it wasn't balanced to begin with. The benefits were one-sided!

With that being said, the most significant sacrifices you'll always have to make is within YOU. My mentor Dr. Shaw always says, "Don't eat according to your desires; eat according to your destiny." In other words, sometimes you must sacrifice what you want at the moment because it may not be conducive to your pipe dream. You can't accept every invitation to go turn up when you have things to do. You can't hang out as late as you'd like to when you have to get up early the next day. You can't date just anyone you're attracted to without knowing if they'll be a blessing or a burden. The same way a natural diet can contribute to your body's shape, your desires can shape the roads of your journey. A poor diet slows you down and causes fatigue. Poor decisions can turn a 40-day process into a 40-year wilderness. Sacrificing momentary desires avoids unnecessary detours. Ask any adult who's been around the block a few times.

THE DEFINITION: **Punctuality** - The state, quality, or *habit* of being on time.

The original meaning of punctual described a puncture made by a surgeon. I love this visual of surgeons because there's a difference between elective surgery and emergency surgery. Elective surgery is planned out. The date and time are set, which gives the surgeon and their team time to prepare. On the other hand, emergency surgery must happen right away to save a life, so there's much more pressure. Both require surgeons to open a human body and make the best decision for treatment. The difference is the surgeon performing emergency surgery is more likely to miss a step or two because he/she has less time to prepare to operate, increasing the likelihood the patient won't make it.

Give yourself room to plan, so you're not always in a rush! You're bound to miss or forget something along the way that can be so little but makes a big deal. Punctuality involves being precise about SMALL points and making a big deal out of minor details. Being punctual is even used concerning grammar. Punctuation gives accuracy to the thought, statement, or question. You want to hit the mark with accuracy in everything you commit to, and it starts with small habits.

The adjustment from tardy to punctual does not have to be this seismic shift, as many of my students presume it to be whenever we start this conversation. Make it a habit to put your keys, wallet/purse, and travel essentials in the same place all the time, so you're not scrambling in the morning looking for them. Check the train/bus schedule and choose the ride that will get you there BEFORE time.

Limit yourself to ONE snooze hit on your alarm clock. I can go on and on with examples, but YOU know where your struggle is regarding time management. Identify that struggle and commit to breaking the poor habits that prevent you from being on time!

II. INTEGRITY

Decoded

Home is our first habitat. It serves as our first teacher and place of development, shaping how we relate to people and perceive any situation. The way we perceive money, relationships, communication methods, conflict, and overall human interaction is influenced by the home we grew up in. It's important to note that the concept of home can be something different for everyone. Home could be a two-parent household, single-parent household, or what we call the system (orphanage, foster care, adoption, group home, etc.). Therefore, I believe introspection is necessary. It gives perspective to the issues we face the most. Whatever we do, that is habit-forming, good or bad, began from what we saw and learned at home. This is why certain traits we possess are called habits. Some of those habits include being emotionally unavailable, the inability to deal with conflict, poor spending practices, insecurities, challenging authority, trust issues, tardiness, hygiene, ineffective communication, just to name a few. Such habits that affect our interaction with humanity are difficult to confront because we developed them in our first habitat, called home. Therefore, we believe it is harmless until we have an encounter that may challenge that perception.

Exposure allows you to see things from a different perspective. As we grow in age and experience, we're influenced by home and school, teams, organizations, workspace, spiritual practice, and overall pop culture. These communities expose us to different people, thoughts, and concepts that may challenge what we've learned at home – for better or for worse.

Each community we're a part of has its own set of codes in which they operate. It's their integrity! A family example would be "what goes on in this house stays in this house." Anyone in the family who irresponsibly puts the family business out in the streets would likely hear the phrase "we don't do that in this family." That is because you've now compromised the integrity of the family and need to be held accountable.

Schools have a code of conduct for the students to abide by. When there's an infraction, disciplinary action is taken to maintain the integrity of that school. I believe public schools need to figure out an alternative to suspension, but that's conversation for another day or book.

Companies have policies and procedures for their employees to abide by. Any employee engaging in behavior that's noncompliant with those policies should be held accountable to maintain that company's integrity.

Socially, there are codes like "girl code" and "bro code." These are a set of do's and don'ts among friends, which may vary among friendship circles. A popular girl AND bro code is DO NOT DATE YOUR FRIEND'S EX! Historically, this choice has been known to compromise friendships' integrity; therefore, it has become an unwritten rule with colorful consequences.

The streets have a code, commonly, DON'T SNITCH! In no way am I encouraging or promoting illegal activity. However, if you're going to make this choice, please understand what your makeup is. I've seen too many people I grew up with making this choice without fully comprehending this code. Are you capable of keeping your mouth shut even if you're presented with an offer to reduce or erase your sentence? Recording artist Keen Streetz said it best when he wrote, "the streets ain't for everybody, that's why they made sidewalks!"

It is important to understand how every community you're a part of operates, so you're able to maintain their integrity, which involves respecting the space you're in!

1. Your job is not your house.
2. Your school is not a space to turn up.
3. Your home is not in the streets.
4. The streets are not a country club.

You don't have the liberty to do whatever you want, wherever you want! Every community we're a part of has the potential to challenge our perception. Although these institutions should never be the total of who we are, they can contribute to our standard of living and how we interact with others.

Climate Change

As an actor, I love improvisation classes. One of my favorite improv exercises is a game called Hitchhiker. It is an exercise where three people are in a make-believe car with four chairs, and they're all having a conversation. The thing is, they're all conversing with the same personality. The driver notices a hitchhiker on the side of the road and pulls over to pick him/her up. The hitchhiker then enters the vehicle, starting a new conversation with a whole new personality. Everyone else in the car takes on that same personality while engaged in the conversation. The driver comes up with a reason to pull over for the next hitchhiker/personality. The driver exits, the hitchhiker enters with his/her personality, and everyone shifts their seating. This allows everyone a chance to bring their personality to the experience. What makes this improv so entertaining is the fact that you have no idea where it'll go. Each personality that enters the car brings a new dynamic to the scene. Everyone in the vehicle must adjust to what YOU step in with.

Hitchhiker is a powerful illustration of integrity. When you know who you are, you don't allow environments to change you. YOU change the environment! Now let's be clear, this is not a license to just say and do whatever you want wherever you go. This is a plea to stop conforming to everyone and everything around you for some form of acceptance. Just because it's popular doesn't mean it's productive! When entering an environment that does not align with your core values, you have the right to set the tone for how you want to be treated. Humanity is wired to adjust to what's consistent. The behavior, attitude, demeanor, energy that you regularly give off, whether negative or positive, is what people will adapt to and will therefore treat you accordingly.

There's a difference between a thermometer and a thermostat. A thermometer changes based on the temperature of the room, while a thermostat SETS the temperature. Some people are like thermometers. They change based on where they are or who they're around. When they're around this group of friends, they act one way and totally different when they're in the presence of another group. We call those people "wishy-washy," "some-timey," or "flakey" because they change like the weather. It's important not to cast judgment on these people because they may very well be suffering from an identity crisis, which makes them look for acceptance from anyone willing to give it. This is why self-identity is the key to acceptance. Knowing who you are empowers you to set the temperature for any space you enter. Once you accept your flaws and embrace your qualities, you'll develop an uncompromising approach to life.

For this reason, you don't need people to sign off before you take off! Once you've discovered who you are, live by specific codes, and are morally sound, you DO NOT need permission to live what you love! Self-discovery and self-acceptance allow you to stay the course en route to your pipe dreams, especially when you mess up. And trust me, you will make a BUNCH of mistakes along the way. It's ok! Stand firm in the roots you have in the ground from the struggles you've already endured so that you can produce wherever you are planted. Every tree planted was intended to produce something of value to the one who planted it. God planted you in the environment you grew up in so you could present something valuable to those who may not understand your worth. Your job is not to decrease your value to adjust to their ignorance but increase their understanding by what you consistently produce. This even applies to when you get your foot in the door of your pipe dream. Do not compromise your integrity for your industry. Your industry's pressures will never be stronger than your roots in the ground that got you there.

<u>Price Tag</u>

Integrity serves as an amplifier to the best parts of your character and blasts it through subconscious speakers. It lets everyone in the room know that you're compassionate, engaging, present, and have many excellent qualities to offer before you even say a word. It speaks to your value or worth in the eyes of your audience. In fact, it puts a high price tag on you that the average person perceives they cannot afford. And anything someone believes they can't afford, they'll try to bargain. Unfortunately for them, your integrity won't allow you to reduce your price!

Think about high-end brands, for example. You rarely see Louis Vuitton, Versace, Prada, Chanel, and other brands in that price range go on sale. They've already determined their value and set the price for their consumers. If material things rarely go on sale, why should you? Your integrity is worth more than any brand on the market! Do not allow what others can't afford to reduce your value. This is inclusive of every relationship from family to friends, co-workers, and even entanglements. Your integrity is your value, and it is not on sale! Be clear about what you're willing and not willing to do. Your yes is yes, and your no is no! Do not panic when your circle starts to shrink as you grow. Everyone can't afford to be in your space when you're on a mission, and you shouldn't apologize for that. The higher you raise your standard of living and practice respectable ways of treating people, the smaller your **circle** will become. Your value is not priced by the number of followers you have on social media, but by the integrity you refuse to compromise.

Mask On

Covid-19 has had us all adjust to a life of wearing masks. Our government mandate, or at least states with some form of leadership, is to wear a mask in public settings. At first, many of us were bothered by this mandate. Masks are uncomfortable, not to mention hideous to walk around the streets wearing. However, I noticed a growing number of the public began to adhere to these mandates when the masks became customized. Creative people and companies produced masks that varied in size, shapes, colors, and designs to customize this survival method. So much so that masks became a stylish accessory. I believe this made people more comfortable to wear them more consistently and confidently in public. Keep in mind the goal of the masks was to aid in our survival through the pandemic.

In your quest for self-identity, you have the right to customize the accessories needed for YOUR survival. Before COVID-19, we were always in some form of pandemic. From pandemics of dysfunctional families, generational cycles, trauma from childhood abuse, social inequality, police brutality, educational and poverty gaps. To simply be black in America, we've all found ways to survive our social and personal pandemics. What gives us comfort and confidence through these pandemics is the ability to customize our survival methods. Since our emancipation from slavery, we've influenced every art form through our customized masks. From our out of the box fashion statements to our controversial music, colorful slang, and overall influence on pop culture, we thrive in the realm of adaptability!

Uniquely, YOU possess the same ability. Remember, building integrity is a road to self-discovery or a self-identity journey (whichever sounds better). It is vital to find survival methods that are suitable for you to adapt to.

So, go ahead and change your hairstyle if it makes you feel comfortable, and style yourself in unorthodox outfits if you please. Create a new language to articulate your pain through poetry and music. THIS IS HOW HIP-HOP BEGAN! Creativity takes on a life of its own during times of uncertainty. Your struggle gives you the license to create!

I took an improv class back in college, and we did an exercise called "Mask Work." It is known to free the actor's body for the development of the character. Mask Work's objective is to help the actor make new discoveries to the way you say your lines and the body language that takes form. In other words, your mask, your customized method for survival, can help shape the person you're trying to become. It allows you to focus on YOU while you search for YOU. Your mask makes you look different from what people are used to. "You're acting different," "you funny style," "you think you're better," "you changed on us," etc. These are statements you'll hear during your discovery. It doesn't matter. DO NOT take your mask off until you feel it's safe!

The Definition: **Integrity** - Firm adherence to a code of values, especially moral or artistic.

Stick to your guns! When you know who you are, you're less likely to conform to beliefs, behaviors, and ideologies that contradict your values—honor, and respect to every community, institution, and family you're a part of.

Integrity can be a lonely road at times, but you'll always attract what you give off. Although people may not support you and your journey, you can still support people and show love without expectations. Expectations can get your feelings hurt. If your support is reciprocated, then consider it a bonus and appreciate it. Avoid playing politics by supporting people just because you know you have something coming up and would like their support too. That's manipulation, and you should never manipulate support. When people genuinely rock with what you're doing, they'll put forth the energy to your momentum. When they feel it, they just feel it. If they don't, you'll know. And you should learn to be ok with that.

I've learned something recently that helped me manage my associates, friends, and even family expectations. Expecting YOU from other people is an unfair burden to place on anybody. People rarely show up for you the same way you show up for others. I'm proud to say that I have an AMAZING support system. However, I've found myself sometimes disappointed because I expected them to show up for me with the same zeal I would for them. That was so selfish on my part! It's not that they didn't support or show love. It wasn't done how I would do it.

EVERYONE IS BUILT DIFFERENT! Everyone's contribution is based on capacity. Therefore, there's always a limit to how far someone can go for you. There was a point where I started measuring how much I would contribute to supporting someone based off how far they have gone to help me in the past. What's crazy is that I realized how much that attitude drained me even more than the disappointment of their past contributions. I forced my approach, and I did not feel like myself. I was compromising my integrity. Ultimately, I experienced a change in my perception and this allowed me to manage my expectations better.

Integrity is from the math term integer, which is defined as a whole number without fractions. Trauma, family history, heartbreak, disappointments, and life, in general, can break you into pieces you didn't even know could be broken. Integrity is the glue that helps you hold it together when you could easily fall apart. Be one with yourself, your beliefs, and your never-ending growth. Your integrity ensures no period of your life will have the power to leave you broken.

III. PURPOSE

Soul Power

There's more to life than just meeting obligations. Once you become an adult, your life typically revolves around responsibilities. The weight of those responsibilities dramatically increases once you have dependents (significant other, children, family members, etc.). It's one thing to struggle on your own while you're single with no kids. That struggle hits differently when you have a family to feed. Your day-to-day schedule becomes a routine built around survival. You and your partner, or just you as a single parent/caretaker, have been taking micro doses of anxiety for so long, you don't realize you fit the bill for a mental illness evaluation. It's those moments where you step out of your anxiety-fueled hustle and say to yourself, 'THIS CAN'T BE LIFE!' There has to be more to life than just bills on top of bills. Rent, utilities, food, and transportation, just to name a few, should NOT be this difficult to maintain! Not to mention the little humans you created.

At this point, your soul has something to say about all of this. You start to tell yourself things like, "I have more to offer than this job allows me to showcase." If you're a student, it sounds more like, "What do any of these classes have to do with my interests?" It's in these moments your soul wants to be included in your routine. For the most part, our bodies participate in our daily routine, but our souls are disconnected. You're physically present at school or that job but mentally and emotionally checked out. We're sort of like the walking dead. We just show up and go through the motions of these obligations. But we still have a soul.

A soul is defined as emotional or intellectual energy. It is the essence of who we are in pure form and the center of our decision making. The truth is our soul has not left our body, as it does with the dead. It's just locked up in our routine prison of survival, screaming to be let out. And any living thing that's caged will periodically cry out to be released. Living like this brings out the worst in us. It's why some of us walk around with an attitude or exude negative energy. It's because the true essence of who we are is locked up in survival. This is where we may display "animalistic behavior" and are always on edge. When you live with your back against the wall, you'll always scratch and claw instead of embrace and love. It's those introspective moments that make you see the internal warfare you've been subconsciously fighting for way too long. This is where your soul screams and begs for release from the survival prison it's been caged in. If only you could do what you love for a living! But every time you start to hear your soul speak, your struggle makes you store it back to where you've been hiding it.

I advise you to take some time to listen on the next go-round. Your soul speaks the loudest when it sees a reflection of itself. I'll talk more about this in **Muses**. When you see someone thriving in the same industry where you're gifted, your soul recognizes that activity and is desperate to be involved.

One of my go-to motivational songs is called "Bring Me To Life" by Evanescence. The opening verse states,

"How can you see into my eyes like open doors, leading you down into my core, where I've become so numb without a soul, my spirit's sleeping somewhere cold, until you find it there and lead it back home."

This is what your soul sounds like when you come face to face with where you belong. It recognized the activity it was created to engage.

Every time I'm watching one of my favorite actors or even just an excellent performance, I get so lost in the moment that I start seeing myself playing the role. I'd then go off into imagining the entire process:

- ✓ Auditioning for the part
- ✓ The phone call received from my agent telling me I booked the part
- ✓ Meeting my cast members for the first time
- ✓ Doing table reads with the director and scene partners
- ✓ Hair and makeup
- ✓ Wardrobe

- ✓ The multiple takes of each scene
- ✓ The last day of the shooting
- ✓ The promotional tours
- ✓ TV/radio interviews, red carpet events, and screening premiers
- ✓ My outfits for the red carpet and award show(s) that will follow
- ✓ ALL the way down to the acceptance speech I'll give once I win my category

Then I snap back to reality with my soul having had the chance to breathe and stretch, even for a moment.

Now, in the past, I would stop myself from going down this imaginary path because that negative voice in my head would say, "what if you never make it?" and the feeling of that thought is indescribable. However, I've learned to embrace these moments because I realized my soul truly comes alive by allowing myself to go there. I'm pushed harder to give the best performances I possibly can during my real auditions as they come. The more I see myself on screen, the more real it becomes for me. This holds true with all my gifts. Youth development, motivational speaking, and all my creativity allows me to see my current jobs (yes, plural) as just a temporary means to an end. That perspective is vital for my headspace and daily approach to the monotony that comes with survival. When you're crystal clear on the life you know you were created to live, you can better manage your obligations until you get your breakthrough. With this kind of clarity, it's challenging for you to accept a life of normalcy.

Jay-Z said it best on the song "Can I Live" from the classic Reasonable Doubt album; "I'd rather die enormous than live dormant." In other words, your soul would rather depart from your body than live in a cage of survival. This is a realization most people come to between the ages of 40-65, where they look back on how fulfilled their life could've been if they pursued their pipe dreams. This reflection is a contributor to what they call a midlife crisis.

One of the signs of a midlife crisis is the impulsive need to do what you loved to do before your life became burdened with obligations. Some people go back to school to finish what they started, some open a business from an idea they've always had, and simply overall give attention to their interests. If you've ever watched The Fresh Prince of Bel-Air, you'll see the perfect example of this, even from someone highly successful. It was the episode in Season Two where Aunt Viv turned 40 and realized how much dancing was a part of who she was but neglected for years to take care of her family. She went to an audition, was pretty rusty and couldn't keep up. But on her second go-round, she got BUSY!! (If you know, you know.) The highlight of that episode for me was her response when her family told her to take it easy. She said, "Take it easy? I took it easy 20 years ago when I got that teaching degree. I don't want to take the comfortable road anymore. No one is going to stop me from being a dancer! Now, there's an audition in three weeks, and I'm going to take every class I can. I'm going to show the world that Vivian Banks can dance!" It gave me chills watching it recently on HBO Max because it felt like her soul was finally set free after all these years!

This means IT'S NEVER TOO LATE to pursue your Pipe Dream. However, we can learn from these experiences and not wait for a midlife crisis experience to wake up our souls. Allow yourself to go to that place when your soul starts to speak. The more you see and feel it, the more steps you'll take to make it happen. As a result, you'll be in a better headspace to endure the process en route to purpose.

Choosy

You don't get to choose purpose. It already chose you from birth. But you can identify it in different frames of your life. I believe in the idea that nothing just happens, or "everything happens for a reason." A significant turning point in my life occurred during my time in Cali. I was a student-athlete playing football for Southwestern College in San Diego. I majored in theater, so the highlight of my days was football practice and rehearsal for whatever production I'd find myself in. Until this point, I thought my sole purpose in life was to entertain, perhaps in the NFL, TV/Film, or both. I just knew those two areas of entertainment were what I'd be doing for the rest of my life. In the middle of all of this, I attended a church in the Southeast section of San Diego called Faith Tabernacle. I joined this particular church because I thought the Pastor was surprisingly relevant and the messages connected with where I was spiritually, mentally, and emotionally.

One day Pastor Adrian approached me and asked if I would lead the youth department. The former youth leader had moved, so the position had been vacant for some time. I wasn't sure what to say because I didn't see that coming. When I asked, "why me," He said, "you have a heart for young people. The way you interact with them is from a real place. Plus, you're not far from their age. You can relate to them better than most." I agreed to do it, and I have to say that was one of the best decisions I ever made. Serving in that way gave me a great sense of purpose. I always knew I loved kids but didn't know how good my relationships were with them until I stepped into the role. It wasn't so much the administrative responsibilities that were so fulfilling (I hate administrative work). It was the real-life issues they came to me with. They would talk to me about family issues they were dealing with, academic struggles, insecurities, social acceptance, questions about dating, and all the teenage drama you could think of. Some of their parents would call me if they had a difficult time getting through to their son or daughter at the time.

Of course, at 20 years old, I didn't always have the right answer, so I would reach out to Pastor A for advice on what to say. Ultimately, I just knew seeing the youth prosper became an area of fulfillment for me. From that point on, youth development has been a significant part of my life.

From the type of jobs I applied to, all the way to me starting my non-profit organization for the youth, this experience pulled out something in me I didn't know I possessed: the ability to motivate and inspire young people.

With that being said, none of this would've happened if I had a hand in choosing the process. Towards the end of my senior year in high school, I signed a letter of intent to play football for Robert Morris University in Pittsburgh, PA, through a package of scholarships, grants, and financial aid that the recruiting coach put together. At the time, I was still technically an immigrant in this country, even though I'd been here since I was two years old (Yes, you can scratch your head on that thought). The coach called me one day and said, "Hey Dayo, you forgot to put your social security number in your recruitment form." I told him that I didn't forget; I just don't have one. Of course, he was confused because how can a 17-year-old high school senior not have a social security number, right? I then explained my immigration status to him and how my family and I are still waiting on USCIS to approve my green card application. Disheartened, he said, "Dayo, I'm sorry, but there's nothing we can do for you. Without a social, I can't put you into our system. I'm so sorry man, best of luck to you." When that man hung up the phone, the level of fear, anxiety, and disappointment, I felt all at once could not be reenacted if I tried. All I could think was, what am I going to do now? I had committed to this school because of the football offer, and now I had nowhere to go. I ultimately wound up at Valencia Community College in Orlando, FL. (I may get to how I wound up down there somewhere in this book or the next).

During my first semester, I needed an elective to complete my schedule. On my way to the registration building, I had an open vision. I saw Denzel Washington on a red carpet being interviewed. Visually, I saw Denzel, but symbolically it was me, if that makes any sense.

It was a surreal feeling. I'm a dreamer so I have dreams almost every night and random visions throughout the day. However, this was one of those outer body experiences.

When I snapped out of it, I scratched my head and asked myself if I should take an acting class to complete my requirements. I started thinking about how, in high school, my friends and I would reenact scenes from our favorite movies, being class clowns, and always putting on a show in random moments amongst other friends. Most of the classes offered were already full so I wasn't even sure if an acting class would be available. Bingo, there was a seat available. I took the acting class, fell in love with it, and moved to Cali to pursue a career in it. That is how I got to San Diego and ultimately discovered youth development as part of my purpose.

If I had a hand in choosing my purpose, I NEVER would've chosen this route. I had things all planned out. I would've gone to college on a football scholarship, majored in communications to be an ESPN sports analyst if I didn't make it to the NFL. Youth development was never a part of my plan, but now I wouldn't trade it for anything!

This is what life can do to us sometimes. It'll take us on an unexpected journey, which can be gruesome at times. My Cali experience was no walk in the park at all. Most of that journey, I wouldn't volunteer to repeat. I lived at about seven different addresses fighting to finish what I started. You can have things all planned out, which you should. But when those plans begin to go in a different direction called struggle, pay attention to the varied opportunities present on this road. Purpose doesn't always come while the sun is shining and things are going great. It often shows up in the darkest seasons of your life, where you have no idea of what to do next. Detours are components of getting to destiny!

Simmer

When you discover purpose, you'll never be bound to society's perception of you. The power of purpose liberates you from people's ideas, thoughts, and limits of whom and what you should be. What happens is you begin to operate in a self-controlled climate, where you're too balanced to be bothered.

Picture the temperature gauge on the dashboard of a vehicle. There's an indicator that reads the temperature for that engine. That indicator will let you know if your car is in danger of overheating. If that indicator rises too close to

'H,' you're forced to pull the car over, turn off the engine, let it cool down, and assess the problem – which puts a frustrating pause on your destination.

Purpose is the indicator of your emotional gauge. If you live your life by what other people feel and say about you, you'll always be frustrated and overreact to situations that are unworthy of your attention. Some of us have found ourselves overheating or what we call "blacking out" on people in the past because, yes, they took it there. But also, we had not discovered our purpose at that point. Therefore, there was no indicator telling us to pull over and cool down. Purpose gives you creative control over what you will and will NOT entertain because you've got too much riding on it. It comes with a voice that says, "It's just not worth it."

Last summer, I went to watch my nephew Scottie play a basketball game. There was an outdoor park court, and after the game, people were hanging out, laughing, and joking around. Scottie is a 5-star recruit, so he's a pretty high-profile player with NBA lottery projections. This kid decided to aim all sorts of negative remarks at him. For me, his chatter was out of left field, but apparently, his talking trash to Scottie was all afternoon. They went back and forth with basketball trash talk for a while, which he doesn't back down from (We welcome all smoke in this family ;-)). But things went left when the kid told Scottie, "suck my dick!" during the exchange. If you know my nephew, he is mild-mannered and never loses his temper. That afternoon he lost it! Rightfully so! When he began to raise his voice, I knew this was going downhill, so I ran towards him to keep him from a physical altercation. Before I got there, one of his best friends got in between the two to separate them but then swung on the kid, which further escalated the situation. At this point, I and a few others are directing Scottie toward the parking lot so that he can get away from the madness. When we got to the parking lot, I did my best to remind him that he had TOO MUCH TO LOSE dealing with people like that. But much of my attention went to his friend. I told him that if Scottie was too hot to see he needed to leave the situation, you as his friend, knowing what's at stake, should've removed him from the area immediately! If Scottie would've hit that kid, he most definitely would've pressed charges hoping to cash in on the situation.

Purpose makes both you and those you surround yourself with determine what is and is NOT worth your engagement. The same way an overheated car can blow a head gasket, causing significant delays on your journey and costing unexpected money, is the same way losing your cool to unworthy situations can hinder your road to success. It only takes one moment of an avoidable situation to set you back from what you've been working on. Let purpose be your indicator, and you'll rarely blow a gasket.

Forgive & Foreclose

You have the right to protect your space. Purpose will make you evaluate your relationships with the people in your life.

You'll come to realize that every relationship isn't a healthy contributor to this journey. This includes relationships on every level: family, friends, and various associates (scholastic, professional, organization affiliations). If they can't afford to occupy the space you've created, then they must vacate the premises. Purpose already comes with enough challenges in the form of:

1. Doors being slammed in your face.
2. People telling you no!
3. Less talented individuals getting the opportunities you feel you deserve
4. Working to maintain a steady income while climbing the unstable ladder of your industry.
5. And so many other challenges that are out of your control.

One of the things you have full autonomy over is your mental and emotional space. That is YOUR personal property of which you are the landlord, and every relationship serves as a tenant that pays the rent. Their rent comes in the form of the contributions they're capable of giving. Whether it's unwavering support, financial efforts, or network expansion, they are key contributors to your new space. But something almost always happens when you enter a new area or state of mind. Those who knew you before you discovered purpose might be unable to contribute to that space, which changes the relationship's dynamic.

These challenges usually come in the form of a painful experience caused by someone close to you.

I believe we've all experienced some form of abuse, betrayal, and various forms of trauma that has left a mark so powerful, it's impacted the way we treat others who can safely occupy that space. A child who's been abused verbally, physically, sexually, or emotionally by a parent will likely have issues with authority figures of their same sex. An adult whose trust was betrayed by a friend who shared confidential information might be closed off as well. Another example is a partner being cheated on. In all scenarios, there is the likelihood of becoming emotionally unavailable to anyone due to trust issues.

Purpose makes you identify where these relationships affect your ability to embrace and relate to others that can occupy that space. Whether the trauma occurred in the past or present, converse with the individual(s) to clear the air. Hearing them out may give you clarity as to why they did what they did and could've been a misunderstanding by you. Or it could justify the pain you've been feeling since the offense. This lets the offender know what you've been feeling and opens the door for apologies and making amends for their offense.

HERE'S THE KICKER! Can you accept an apology from an offender that may never say sorry? You'll always remember the pain of the experience but make the conscious decision to leave the impact at your old address. If your offender doesn't own the offense and offer you the apology you deserve, you must be purpose-driven enough to forgive and foreclose. If you ever become bold enough to go to therapy, you'll learn that forgiveness is more for you than for the other person. Forgiveness allows you to heal and move on from the trauma, while foreclosure gives you the power to clear that space for someone who can afford its cost of occupancy.

Every void in your life is meant to be filled. Parentless children will always run into mother and father figures. A friendless person will continually develop unbreakable bonds. A failed romance will soon find enchantment. Trauma from relationships can make you choose to walk alone in those areas, but purpose always comes with a partnership. You can only go so far by yourself. Choose to forgive and foreclose so you can make room for major contributors to your purpose.

Interest

When you have an interest in something, your entire life tends to revolve around it. Your time, schedule, preparation, focus all goes to this interest during that time. My reflection on high school validates this thought for me. Good grades were an interest. Not only because I'm Nigerian and good grades are a prerequisite to keep your life, but up until ninth grade, I had no personal interest in good grades. From 5th grade to 8th, I remember just doing enough to pass my classes and move on to the next grade. That alone should tell you that God is a keeper – I don't know how I'm still alive! Something incredible happened to me during the first marking period of my freshman year. I found out you could walk right out the main entrance anytime you want, and security wouldn't stop you. WHAT??? Such liberty! Such freedom! I, sure enough, took advantage of it. My cut buddies and I left school every day after 3rd period, which was homeroom. This way, we weren't marked absent for the day. We went everywhere from the Popeye's on Guy Brewer, the McDonalds near Merrick, everywhere on Jamaica Ave, and whoever had the "free crib" that day. I was never picked up by truancy, so my only trepidation was running into one of these uncles or aunties from my Nigerian community, who had permission to slap me in the middle of the street, then tell my parents. It was all good until that first marking period report card came in. If memory serves me correctly, I earned 50's (F) from top to bottom. Maybe a couple of 55's (F+). I had a borderline panic attack because I was afraid of my parents' reaction to this. Noticing my anxiety, one of my cut buddies asked me what was wrong. When I explained to him how I'd be walking the green mile that evening, he told me that this is just the first marking period. It's only the third marking period report card that goes out to the parents. After a huge sigh of relief, I looked at those grades again and told myself that I'm better than what the grades showed. I then challenged myself to earn an 80 average for the next marking period. It felt so good seeing that second report card that I wound up doing so for the remainder of my high school years, graduating with an 83 average. What the fear of my parents couldn't do, my interest did! Earning a spot on the principal's honor roll felt right to me, so I chose to stay there. That's the power of interest. Authentic engagement comes when there's a genuine desire!

The same thing happened with basketball. I wasn't like most of my friends who were playing the game since they could walk. I only played toward the end of middle school because they would need one more player. After a while, the game became interesting to me. My competitive spirit came alive, and I would soon realize how much I hated losing. Entering high school, basketball became my life. I was one of those "ball is life" students. My days consisted of practice, tournaments on the weekends, better eating habits (to the best of my ability as a teenager), sneakers to hoop indoors and a separate pair for outdoors, headbands, and everything I could to make playing comfortable for me. I made all the sacrifices physically and monetarily because of this interest. Then came Football around junior year, an interest developed through an introduction. I was asked to join the team because of their desperate need for cornerbacks. I barely even knew what the position was, let alone what it required. As I continued to attend practices my first week, and ultimately my first game, I developed a stern interest in the game. Even though I was still raw and learning its nuances, the desire to compete drove me. Therefore, the skills for my position developed as I learned the game. That off-season, I decided to continue playing football.

I participated in all offseason activities, workouts, meetings, and a program called HSPD (High School Player Development). I even bought a gym membership at St. John's Recreation Center in Brooklyn to begin working on my own. I gained about 10 pounds that offseason heading into my senior year. The work paid off because I began to gain interest from several colleges. I received letters from the University of Virginia, Fordham University, Stonybrook, University at Buffalo, just to name a few. I eventually earned All-Queens honors at the end of the season. I would've been selected All-City if only…. (Maybe I will share in the next book). Football became my life!

Let's not forget about the girls. When I was interested in a girl, I became more detailed with my outfits by ensuring my ironing was perfect. My sneakers were cleaned until they looked new. My dad had many colognes he didn't use, so I would take one or two to keep in my locker to spray on every two to three periods. This way, whenever (if ever), I found the right opportunity to step to her, she could ask what I have on, which makes it easier to "break the ice." And of course, I had to keep a fresh haircut. I had waves at the time, so the routine was one-week haircut, the next week a shape up, and so on. Of course, the teenage chase was always a hit or miss, regardless of preparation. However, I'm glad I missed some of them because they didn't age too well (shade). All of this is to say when you have an interest, your entire life revolves around it. Our years of adolescence displayed the purest form of obsession.

We dwell on the things we really like and have all the energy in the world to go after them. This is what living with purpose looks like. It's not a complicated math problem. It's simply related to your interests. Whatever your interests are, your life has the right to revolve around them. Society and some of our cultures teach us to conform to what they want us to be. For us Nigerians, it's become a doctor, lawyer, or engineer. Outside of that, you're a rebel, vagabond, shame to the family, and many other things we're liable to be dramatically called.

When I got "bit by the acting bug," all I wanted to do from that point on was perform on stage or TV/film. My entire life revolved around acting. I took classes, paid for workshops, attended showcases, and made many sacrifices, including dealing with my family's disapproval at the time because this was my interest! Today I'm proud to say I have credits in film, television, and theater. You have one life to live, and if you ignore your interests, a midlife crisis will be inevitable. I'm not saying life will be peaches and cream once you pursue your interests. You'll most certainly endure hardships. The difference is you'll stick to it because you genuinely have the desire for it.

There's a reason why most degree holders don't work in the industry of their education. There was little to no interest. Most people change their major or outright drop out of school because the course load doesn't feed their curiosity. You're more likely to fight through the challenges of education when it's centered around your interests!

I remember being one of the speakers at a conference a few years ago. My message was about purpose and doing what you love for a living. Not surprising, right? After the conclusion, a woman came to me and said, "I wish my friend's son could've heard your message before he died." When I asked how he died, she said, "His parents killed him." The young man matriculated through college, graduated from medical school, and was at the time doing his residency when he took his own life. In his suicide note to his parents, he stated how much he wanted to pursue a music career (he played the keyboard), but his parents forced him to be a doctor. I am not advocating suicide, but is life even worth living when you can't live with what you love? His soul was probably crying for release through undergrad and med school but forced to stay in its place. Unfortunately, his soul found freedom via tragedy.

Look at interest in terms of money. It is a financial term for growth. Your money accrues interest by staying in an interest-bearing account. The longer it stays, the greater the return. Your area(s) of interest is where you deserve to spend most of your time.

Muse

In 2015, our beloved Kobe Bryant produced a documentary that detailed the rivalries, partnerships, and mentors that helped shape his 18-year career. What stood out to me was acknowledgments of former players such as Larry Bird, Magic Johnson, and Michael Jordan that he looked up to.

He called them his Muses. One of the definitions of muse is "a source of inspiration." Kobe was content with retiring because after winning five championships, "I can sit at the same table as my muses." That kind of inspiration sets the bar for the level of success you're capable of achieving in your industry. What's incredibly amazing to me is your muse is inclusive of yet not exclusive to those you look up to in your industry.

As an actor, I most certainly have gifted actors and actresses that I love and look up to. However, I can include recording artists, producers, preachers, athletes, and other gifted people in that mix. The reason being is their influence transcends their industry. They've managed to master their gifts and venture into different areas of business and entertainment. They were introduced to the world as just a talent, but now they're giving commencement speeches, building studios, writing books, and inspiring well beyond their talent. The byproduct of their gifts is what makes them my muses.

Purpose will have you running from your past and chasing your future at the same time. Whatever you don't want your life to look like takes a back seat to the life you want to emulate. This is where our Muses come in. They give us a constant source of inspiration that we pull from and a standard to uphold in everything we do.

I can name all my muses, but I think it's more important to highlight the common thread amongst all of them. They make me feel comfortable in my skin! Every one of them marches to the beat of their personal drum. They had a thought, concept, vision, or method of approach that wasn't so popular to critics nor fit the social norm; therefore, they revolutionized their profession. I find comfort in my muses every time I think an idea or approach I have will seem "weird" or unaccepted by others. My muses that aren't actors, I don't identify with their talent but their unique ability to not give a damn.

Your muses have a personality trait that connects with yours and serves as a jumpstart to your dead battery. When you see or hear them in their element, it awakens what's already in you, encouraging you to stick to your guns.

One of my favorite scriptures says, "iron sharpens iron." You're already as good as your muses. The truth is you must repetitively fill your day with inspiration that mirrors the lifestyle you desire to live. You already have what they possess to make it happen. You just need to see it in someone else to remind you of the standard they set for you. This way, you'll never be ok with being average in your field. Like Kobe, you won't hang it up until you can sit at the same table as those who inspired you.

The Definition: **Purpose** - the reason behind something or someone's creation.

Mark Twain said, "The two most important days in your life are the day you were born and the day you find out why." The keyword is WHY! We all can say WHO we are by name, WHAT we are by nationality, WHERE we were born, WHEN we were born, and of course HOW we were born. But many of us struggle to understand WHY we were born. I have a couple of questions for you:

1. Why do you love what you love or hate what you hate?
2. Why are certain matters so important to you that seem irrelevant to others?
3. What would you do for the rest of your life, and be fulfilled, if you could get paid for it?

The day you find out WHY you were born is the day you truly start living! Basically, we are just breathing and existing until we begin to live on purpose. One of the greatest songs ever written, in my opinion, is "Why" by Jadakiss. The song poetically details several problems he noticed in society that he felt needed answers. YOU WERE CREATED TO SOLVE PROBLEMS! You are the answer to someone or a group of people's problems. The reason specific issues in your community and society weigh heavily on you is because you have the compassion to contribute to the answer. Both pain and passion are potent emotions. When the pain you feel about certain issues develops into a passion for seeing it change, you're realizing your purpose.

Purpose is an overwhelming passion to aid in a particular struggle. Some people may never be delivered from their struggle until purpose is discovered. Think about it from this perspective:

1. Who's dying because you won't step into your purpose?
2. Who's not going to make it out of their struggle because you'd rather conform to society's view of success?
3. What issues will remain the same because you're running from your calling?
4. Who's dream will never come to fruition because you ignore your convictions?

For clarity's sake, I'm not saying you're going to save the world! Purpose doesn't make you a superhero but rather a connected human being whose influence knows no boundaries. You have NO IDEA what kind of impact you can make once you tap into your purpose. Muhammad Ali didn't plan to be the defiant civil rights leader we know him to be today. He was faced with a challenging moment and stepped up to the plate despite public backlash. When asked to fight in the Vietnam War via the draft, he had the courage of conviction to say no. He was quoted saying,

"My conscience won't let me go shoot my brother, or some darker people, or some poor, hungry people in the mud for big powerful America. And shoot them for what? They never called me nigger, and they never lynched me.

They never put any dogs on me, and they didn't rob me of my nationality, rape, and kill my mother and father – Shoot them for what? How can I shoot them poor people? Just take me to jail."

Faced with a significant fine and imprisonment, he did not back down from his position. The pain he felt for his people here in the US would not allow him to go overseas and inflict that same kind of pain on other people of color. That pain developed into a passion for ending the war and fighting for civil rights here in the US. Even though it cost him his boxing license, in the prime of his career, popularity in the media, and millions of dollars, he didn't waver on his position. That kind of pride and conviction only comes when you discover your purpose. You're determined to see the problem through! Ali's conviction was ultimately overturned, and his boxing license reinstated after three difficult years. The impact of Ali didn't come from his success in the ring but from the day he denied his draft into the United States Army. In maybe the darkest season of his life, he found his purpose.

Purpose is rarely discovered when your life is on cruise control. The discovery usually comes in the darkest seasons of life when faced with challenges beyond your comprehension. When the pain of those challenges develops into a passion for eradicating the problem, then you may have found your purpose. You may not have a say in the struggles you encounter, but you do have the capacity to contribute to its solutions. I just believe if we live through something, we are responsible for leaving our impact on it. Purpose will make you give your struggle as many scars as it's given you.

Purpose is discovered through exposure to different thoughts, challenges, ideologies, and ways of life we've experienced. That predicament, that circumstance, or that challenge gives your soul a burden you can't shake.

For my young people, it's using what you love to solve a problem that you hate. You love doing things, but some things in your life turn your stomach every time you see them. If it bothers you to see homeless people in the street, you can get into real estate and purchase a property to provide housing for the homeless. If you're an athlete with pro potential, use that platform to solve a problem that you hate. If the violence in your community is your burden, then you can use your pro money to build community centers to provide a safe space for the teenagers in your community. Whether you're into technology, science, the arts, media, medicine, or athletics, take what you love and use it to solve a problem you hate. Purpose gives direction to your gift(s) and helps narrow down career choices. Without purpose, all we'll do is experiment with degrees, jobs, and relationships, trying to figure out where we fit in life. What is the result? Many are knee-deep in student loan debt with degrees not used. Many of us work at jobs that don't pay us what we're worth. Past relationships only went as far as they did.

Failed experiments, including dating, are a result of no fulfillment! We will waste so much time and money with experiments when the truth is, purpose can shape our understanding of why we're gifted with particular talents and have a burden for certain issues. Our education, career, and relationships have a greater success rate when pursued through the realm of purpose.

IV. EXCELLENCE

Commitment

If you can walk away from it anytime you FEEL, then it's not a commitment...it's a side piece. You're not always going to be in the mood to get the job done. You're human. We all have moments when we're tired, overwhelmed, discouraged, frustrated, and overall emotional with everything else we have going on in our lives. It would be great if bills, deadlines, school assignments, dependents, and obligations were put on pause until you commit to a goal. All your obligations come with levels of emotions you wish would take a back seat to your purpose. But your emotions sit in the passenger seat right next to you. You can choose to pull over every time they have something to say, which is what the average person does because we give more attention to our emotions than we do our commitments. And that is perfectly fine if you're ok with being average. But if you want to stand out amongst your peers, then your level of commitment must override emotions. Do not allow yourself to be your biggest obstacle. The external hurdles you'll have to go through are challenging enough. Don't add your unreliable emotions to the equation.

You started the journey in the first place because you saw something that woke up your soul. You had a vision of something that satisfies a specific desire. For this reason, you committed to pursuing what you envisioned. Remember what it looked like in your mind, thus the importance of vision boards. We all need a daily reminder of why we're grinding the way we are; otherwise, we'll run out of gas. The more you see it, the more tangible it becomes to you, which allows your passion to be the primary emotion speaking to you. Vision fuels the passion needed for commitment.

When passion starts to speak, your obsession overrules all objections. That includes objections from your emotions, your doubts, your fears, current situations, etc. Those are just internal. There will be plenty of external objections, including discrimination, bias, favoritism, red tape, and industry politics. People will tell you to be realistic, and it's not possible. They will also say you're "doing the most" and all kinds of negativity from their disbelief. Let your obsession overrule their objections! Excellence in any field of choice is not measured by one's talent and abilities but by their commitment level.

You Get What You Pay For

Everything has a price. Whether you pay monetarily or with other resources, achieving any goal with a level of excellence will cost you SOMETHING! Preparation is your most valuable asset in an excellent market. It is defined as the action or process of making something ready for use or service. Excellence in any arena requires preparation. Athletes prepare for their season during the offseason and prepare for games during practice. If they just showed up to a competition without preparing their bodies and minds, they can be seriously injured or embarrassed. Advertisers prepare their pitch to their clients before they give the green light for the commercial. Entrepreneurs prepare their presentations to investors before they have the meeting. Performing artists repeatedly rehearse with their band, castmates, or group before they hit the stage for the audience. Attorneys prepare their case before presenting to a judge and jury in the courtroom. Everyone has something good to offer, regardless of where they're gifted and talented. It is those who show up prepared that get the results they're looking for. The truth is, you'll spend more time in preparation than you do in performance, from athletes to entertainers, to entrepreneurs, and beyond. Your performance, demonstration, or presentation has a certain amount of time allotted to do your thing. The audience or spectators come for that small amount of time to watch you make it happen. All the hours, days, weeks, months, and years before that are on YOU to prepare for that small window of time.

1. How much time are you committing to your craft?
2. How many hours do you spend developing your gift(s)?

3. How many days a week do you work out?
4. How many books are you reading on your subjects of interest?
5. How many YouTube tutorials are you watching to improve your technique?
6. How many workshops, clinics, intensives, and seminars are you investing in to keep your gift(s) sharp?

These are questions you need to ask yourself if you want to put yourself in a position not only to compete but to separate yourself. The level of success you want to achieve is not set up for the elite but separated BY the elite. The amount of time you spend preparation separates you from those who are more talented than you, come from a better background than you, grew up with more resources than you, and have more connections than you do. You're on a lifetime payment plan with success and will never default on payments when your currency is preparation. Work harder than everyone else during preparation. Examine who's in the race with you and measure their speed. Whoever is in front of you, figure out a way to catch up. Whoever is behind you, figure out a way to create further separation. There's no sweet spot with excellence. You're either prepared, or you'll get embarrassed. Just because you winged it before and got away with it doesn't mean you got it like that. Even a dead clock is right twice a day.

You Wanna Be Tired, Or You Wanna Win?

Yes, I had to come in with all caps for this one. To suffer defeat because of fatigue is straight-up irresponsible. It is your RESPONSI-BILITY to put time, effort, and energy during practice/rehearsal to deliver an excellent performance. That includes performance on stage, the operating room, the courtroom, the basketball court, whatever your platform. Excellence in any field of study can be traced back to fighting fatigue during training.

Let's use basketball for illustration purposes. Any gifted player can put on a show during the first three quarters of a game. It's the excellent ones that perform the best when it counts the most – the 4th quarter! This is not because suddenly, they became magically better during crunch time. The truth is they refuse to let fatigue determine the outcome of the game. When everyone else is slowing down, excellent players shift into another gear of mental toughness, which is only developed during practice. These are the players that fight fatigue during practice. You'll always win the battle against an enemy you're familiar with. Fatigue is not a stranger that surprises you during the game. It is an ugly familiar face that always shows up at practice. The excellent players separate themselves by going harder during drills when fatigue shows up. They sprint when they feel like jogging, talk to themselves to self-motivate, remind themselves of why they're doing this, get in the gym before everyone else, stay after everyone else leaves, and even put in extra time practicing on their own outside of the team's schedule. Excellent players are familiar with fighting fatigue during practice, so it becomes 2nd nature to fight it in the 4th quarter, at crunch time, when everyone else is tapped out! Every time you've witnessed a fantastic performance by an excellent player, it's because they've fought through fatigue during practice!

I believe it was back in 2011. I was training one of the top high school point guards in NYC, CJ Davis, from Molloy HS. Late into the workout, he was utterly exhausted. It was one of those hot and humid New York summer mornings where you step out of the house and start sweating. We'd just finished up a defensive drill when I told him to shoot free throws. Initially, I told him to make ten free throws, and he'll be done for the day. He then told me, "hold up Dayo, let me catch my breath...I'm tired." His fatigue was justified because he had worked extremely hard during this workout. However, I knew his potential was greater than the pain he was feeling at the moment. So, I said to him, "You wanna be tired, or you wanna win? Everyone gets tired in the 4th quarter, but everyone doesn't get to win. Make your choice." He sucked it up, accepted the challenge, and walked over to the free-throw line. I made him a deal to push him even further. The agreement was he had to make five free throws in a row, and then he's done for the day. If he missed one, he'd have to run suicides (a basketball sprint) and then start over. Taking the deepest breath he probably ever took in his life; he made all five free throws! I said to him, "now, don't you ever tell me you lost a game because you were tired."

There will be competition on every level of your craft/career choice. Anything you commit your life to doing successfully, there will be tremendous competition you'll have to fight through to make a name for yourself. I remember watching an interview with Will Smith, and he was asked about his mental approach to success. He said the difference between him and his competition is he's "willing to die on the treadmill." "If you and I were to compete on a treadmill, one of two things is going to happen; either you're getting off first, or I'm going to die." In other words, I'm not going to lose to my competition because I'm tired! The options are winning or dying because I will not disqualify myself! That's the mindset it takes to do things with excellence. Are you willing to put everything you have into what you love to do? Because if you always put your vision on pause due to fatigue, you'll keep setting the table for someone else to eat the meal you've prepared.

The fact is fatigue will always be a factor. Just don't let it become the focus! By the way, fatigue is not only physical, but also mental. When you commit to something and then face a variety of challenges, it can be mentally exhausting, to the point when you say, I'M OVER IT! And that is the moment you must ask yourself, YOU WANNA BE TIRED, OR YOU WANNA WIN? Choose to win.

Winning feels incredible on any level! Decide to see your vision through no matter how you feel at the moment of fatigue. Think about how many times we've failed to meditate, pray, read, workout, or whatever we challenged ourselves to do to get our mind right in the morning because we were too tired. We let ourselves down when we succumb to fatigue. Excellence is a chosen mindset. This mindset is for every level during your process. Every class in school, work assignment, the event for your start-up business, creative session for your project, and every preparatory method for what you're producing, fight that enemy (inner-me) called fatigue, and you'll always distinguish yourself amongst your peers!

The next time you commit to something and fatigue starts to creep in, ask yourself, YOU WANNA BE TIRED OR YOU WANNA WIN?

Allergic To Normal

Anything you're allergic to, you'll break out from. It's normal for you to stress out over contemplating buying what you want. Remember that feeling of worry/anxiety after purchasing an outfit, appliance, or anything that satisfies that desire. Whether you responsibly choose not to buy it because you have other priorities, or you buy it and stress overwhelms you, PLEASE remember that feeling when you're putting in work for what you're trying to accomplish. You want your product or performance to be undeniably great where people will always pay for what you present. Money has always been a factor in our decision making. It's an everyday struggle for us.

Kanye said, "Having money isn't' everything. Not having it is." If you're tired of that feeling of not having it, then break out of the habits and work ethic that keeps you normal or average. We all know that doing the same thing over and over, expecting a different result, is insanity. Our normal is our insanity. When you decide the stated term is no longer good enough for you anymore or isn't producing the results you envision, you've met the prerequisite for excellence. An excellent mindset is the greatest antihistamine for normalcy. This comes with a serious level of commitment because family and friends won't always understand your process, which will result in some criticism. You'll always look foolish to people you used to share standards with because your process is now different. You put more time into what you're doing because you've set a standard of what it should look like. You're not around as much because you're busy making progress towards your goals. You invest more time, effort, and resources than everyone else on the things you value. This kind of behavior will always open doors for the ones closest to speak negatively about you. "He's acting differently." "She thinks she's better than us." "Who do you think you are?" are some of the rhetoric that will come in your direction.

Just remember this: it's not your job to justify your new habits so you can live the lifestyle you desire. It is your right to grace them with results! If what they speak doesn't match what you see, you reserve the right to separate until the goal is met. We don't get to see actors at rehearsal because we'll criticize the process before the performance. We don't get to watch recording artists record their music because we can't endure the hours and hours of studio sessions and singing do-overs. We're not invited to science labs during invention cultivation because we have a microwave mindset, and they're going to be in there for a while. YOUR BEHIND THE SCENES IS TOO MUCH FOR THE AVERAGE PERSON TO CONCEPTUALIZE! You can't invite people to what they can't understand.

Purpose doesn't invite everyone to the process; it only needs an audience for the performance. To produce excellence at any level, your process will be ugly and full of failures. When YOU know what the finished product should look like, you'll stick to it. Stop backing out of what you envision for yourself to fit in or be accepted. There's an audience of strangers waiting to pay for what you're capable of producing. Yes, you'll lose some friends on this journey. You'll most certainly lose some family. Denzel said, "Your own family will talk shit about you when you're in the process of breaking all their generational curses. This ain't for the weak." Loss and separation are expected results of excellence. You have too much value in you to just accept the average. You deserve to live the life you see and envision for yourself, but you must become allergic to normal to see it through. You have standards, and that's ok! Make no apologies about that. You're not arrogant, just ALLERGIC! When you break out of normalcy, you'll always deliver an excellent performance that demands an encore! That's when the big bucks start rolling in! (If you know, you know)

Network

"If you want to go fast, go alone. If you want to go far, go together." I want to emphasize the vitality of your village on your journey. Yes, you may start alone and by yourself, because there's no buy-in from immediate family and friends. But along the way, you'll meet some incredible people who'll take pride in supporting you without asking for anything in return.

I'm creative, so I just want to hit the go button and make all my ideas happen! I see something in my mind and just want to do it. My series of failures have taught me that sustained success only occurs when creativity meets administration. When you're a creative, it is a LIFELINE to be surrounded by administrative people and vice versa. There are very few people I know who both are gifted in creativity as well as administration. I am NOT one of those people! My administrative skills are a work in progress. Fortunately, I'm surrounded by so many administrative people. Almost everyone in my circle is administrative, organized, and incredibly resourceful. I've learned the power of administration gives structure to your ideas. It's like the human body, which is beautifully made. Our soul contains our thoughts, ideas, and creativity. But it is our physical body that gives movement to those thoughts. Our body consists of bone structure, tissues, organs, skin, and multiple functioning systems. If any of these systems malfunction, then our ideas are limited in execution. Our physical body serves as the administrator to the creativity of our souls. One cannot function at an optimum level without the other. This is what it looks like to have a strong community. Everyone contributes something valuable to your vision. Particularly in the areas of your weakness!

I am blessed to be surrounded by my weakness! I remember back in 2014 when I decided to start GPA officially. I had notes in my phone of the name of the company (different name at the time. Thank God I changed it!), the population I wanted to serve, the artists I wanted to work with, the type of workshops I wanted to provide the youth, and the principles I wanted them to walk away with. In my greenlight brain, I was ready to launch the program! I called my bro Vic who's a choreographer, and we started planning for a launch date. THANK GOD it didn't happen that way! I mentioned the idea to one of my mentors, Dr. Shaw. He asked if we could meet to discuss details and so he could support. I threw all my creative ideas at him during this meeting, and he threw back ADMINISTRATION! He loved the concept of what I was doing but knew it lacked sustainable structure. In this meeting, Dr. Shaw gave me a blueprint for SUSTAINED success. He told me:

1. I needed to incorporate GPA as an official business.
2. Apply for a 501(c)(3) non-profit status to establish funding eligibility.

3. Create a GPA page on all social media platforms
4. Purchase a domain name while building a website.
5. Open a business account.
6. Structure the workshops to run weekly instead of monthly
7. Tie the core values within each workshop so the youth are empowered with principles as well as arts enrichment
8. Among more detailed advice to operate as a legitimate business!

He even gave me the card of a non-profit law firm that would help me file my documents to the state properly. I was given a wealth of information within one hour! The biggest takeaway from that meeting was the structure of my core values. I told him the principles I've adopted on my journey and would like to teach the youth *purpose, excellence, integrity, and punctuality,* in that order. After looking up at the ceiling in his creative juice mode, mumbling words, he said, "pipe.... PIPE DREAMS! You're giving them tools to achieve their pipe dreams." Sheeeeeeeeeeeeesh!!!! All I could say was WOW! He rearranged the order of the principles to create an acronym. It was reminiscent of the scramble board on Soul Train (Children, Google is your friend). This is what happens when creativity meets administration! Had I not said anything, I would've launched this great idea that would eventually crumble because I lacked the structure to sustain it. Which brings me to this point: Always talk about what you do! Make your vision so clear to your village that they pick it up and run with it! If your vision remains in your head, then you'll only daydream. But when you talk about what you're doing with trusted associates, you'll attract collaborations you didn't even know you needed.

This brings me to another point: BE FLEXIBLE! Your way isn't the only way. We know the old saying, "there's more than one way to skin a cat." Be open to different methodologies of getting the job done. Your network of trusted friends, family, and associates will offer tools to make YOUR vision a reality – if you let them!

I remember telling Robin, one of the godparents of my daughters, about GPA. She said, "This sounds great. You need a proposal." She asked me all the details of what I wanted to do and then drafted my first proposal on the spot! Of course, it's been revised and updated as the years went on, but it was the paperwork I submitted that got me my very first workshop at P.S. 43 in Far Rockaway. You won't know how strong your network is until you announce your vision. You WILL get some negativity and pessimism. It's inevitable. But the support you'll receive will blow your mind! I've received so many casting notices for auditions because of my network. I've been invited to speak at workshops, seminars, protests, and so many youth-related events because my village understands my vision and is willing to connect me to opportunities that serve my purpose. I've gone farther with my network than I could've ever gone by myself!

The Definition: **Excellence** - the quality of being outstanding or extremely good.

Excellence is a LIFESTYLE! Apply this mentality to everything you do. Even the little things like cleaning up your room or showing up to work on time. This way, you aim to be excellent in every aspect of your life. It's like muscle memory. The more you do it, the more natural it becomes. If you're only attempting to achieve excellence when you know you'll have an audience, you're choosing a mighty struggle. Everything you're doing for that particular moment will be aimed at pleasing the spectators instead of satisfying YOUR vision or personal goal. Excellence must be internal. It's a mentality you must maximize every opportunity without focusing on what's missing. Focus on what's available and exhaust it!

There's someone out there missing an ingredient or component that you have and WISH they could have what you do. There's someone without legs who used to have them. If they could have legs again for just one day, they'd run across state lines like Forrest Gump. There's someone who has brain damage who used to have a normal functioning brain. If they had the chance at your brain function for one more day, they'd maximize their thoughts and ideas to create the impossible. There's someone who can't hear, see, feel, taste, or touch anymore. The bottom line is excellence is MAXIMIZING what you have! Use it until you can't use it anymore.

I used to think successful people came up with these complex ideas that only special people had the talent for. The truth is they use simplicity to create their masterpiece. The best of the best pull from their experience and paint it on their personal canvas. When Kevin Hart produced "Laugh At My Pain," he simply took his experience and used them as jokes his audience could relate to. When Jay-Z wrote, "Can I Live," he took his experience and recorded a masterpiece his audience can relate to. When Will Smith performed his iconic "How come he don't want me, man?" scene on the Fresh Prince of Bel-Air, it resonated in so many homes because many can relate to that. Stop over-complicating your genius!

Don't wreck your brain trying to find the most elaborate/exclusive way to present your product. It's exclusive to you because it's YOUR experience. You have everything you need to write songs, portray a character, produce your film, start your business, launch your clothing line, develop an app or discover cutting edge technology. Moreover, you were created to excel in YOUR industry with the simplicity of YOUR conviction. If it's genuinely your desire to do it, then do it with conviction. That conviction is what makes you put everything you have into it, therefore presenting it with excellence! The root word for excellence is the Latin word excellere, which means to surpass. Embrace the spirit of excellence and watch how many people you surpass on your way to destiny. You'll know you're operating in excellence when you're one of the top five people your associates think about when your gift is needed.

OUTRO

You Know Why I'm Here

Former NFL running back Marshawn Lynch, aka "Beast Mode," was not a fan of the league-mandated interviews. All he wanted to do was mind his business and play football. As a professional athlete, one of the obligations is to make yourself available for interviews and press-related matters for the league. Beast Mode could care less until the NFL dug into his pockets. Lynch was fined by the league every time he missed an interview. As we all know by now, money talks. Knowing he had to show up for interviews, press conferences, etc., to avoid further fines, he made himself available on his terms. He began to show up, making a statement that would ultimately go viral and become a meme. When asked specific questions about the game he just played, he would respond, "You know why I'm here." Every reporter that asked any question was answered with, "You know why I'm here." This statement is a disposition we've all experienced when we're mandated to do something we could care less about. Particularly at work or in school. What's interesting about the statement is how we can use it to speak to our apathy. When it comes to your place of employment or school of training, talk to yourself every time you feel like quitting. Tell yourself, "You know why I'm here."

If I have any regrets about my journey, it would be my stubbornness toward keeping a job. When acting became my number one priority, I refused to let my work schedule interfere with my auditions. I didn't understand the totality of what it takes to compete in this industry. Everything requires an investment. Headshots, workshops, training, seminars, gas, food, and the overall cost of living! If I could provide some wisdom for any young artist at this moment, I'd say SECURE YOUR POCKETS! You always want to be in a position to finance your vision. Having faith in your vision is admirable and, quite frankly, a necessary component to your pipe dream(s). But please understand, faith and finance play on the same team. You may not like your job or some aspects of what's required of you, but practice telling yourself, "You know why I'm here." When it's all said and done, acknowledging why you get up and grind on that job gives you the motivation necessary to keep it until a more favorable opportunity presents itself.

Use your job as your corporate sponsor or primary investor to your pipe dream(s). Although people will offer to help you out and provide their services pro-bono, nothing is like paying for what you want to be created or completed. You'll know what you've paid for and have the right to expect it done according to YOUR timeline.

Taking this approach can give you more peace at your workplace, limiting the stress factors that stifle your creativity. When you have the funds to finance what you envision, you'll bypass the disappointments that accompany free services.

Kill Or Be Killed

We've all been exposed to people who are already where we'd like to be. We religiously listen to their music, read their books, watch their films, or simply keep up with the moves they're making. They look like something we see in ourselves. But based on our present environment, we don't always believe that could be us. Before putting it on paper or a vision board, we must have seen or heard it somewhere. Everything positive you're attracted to serves as snapshots of your future. From the type of artists you listen to, performers you like to watch, books of authors you read, podcasts you subscribe to, and personalities you organically try to emulate, they're all pictures for your vision board. We're attracted to success stories because there's a connection between what they do and what's caged in our souls.

Make the decision today to set your soul free. The power of your decision changes everything around you. Some years ago, I sat in a seminar hearing Financial Advisor Loyan Mensah break down the 'power of decision.' When you look at the word decide, the suffix "cide" in decide means to kill. Pesti-cide means to kill insects and rodents, homi-cide is to kill someone, sui-cide is to kill yourself, and geno-cide kills a group of people.

When you de-cide to live what you love, you kill off every other option. Therefore, failure is undoubtedly NOT an option! To live what you love seems farfetched and borderline impossible. But I'll testify that God lives in the realm of the impossible. He lives for those moments when you're faced with "how am I going to make this work?" That's when your faith has to kick in because you CANNOT make it work!

I remember when getting my bachelor's degree was no longer pursuant for me. I fell into a dark depression because I've had these plans of getting my degree since I was a teenager. I had it all mapped out, and just like that, it was no longer a reality. I had no idea how I would fit into this competitive world of degree holders. Success seemed impossible. But low and behold, during that span of time, I've been cast for roles on television, played a role in the movie" Freedom" with Cuba Gooding Jr. (currently on Amazon prime video), got married with, and have three beautiful children. I'm an event MC, a non-Profit organizer in youth development, motivational speaker, unofficial life coach, and now a published author with this book.

Trust me, I'm not bragging because I'm far from fulfilling my PIPE Dreams. I'm merely testifying that what I called a nightmare was just a different route to destiny. God knew there was more to me than only fitting into a societal norm. Although acting is my PIPE Dream, I had so much more to offer that I didn't realize until my plans failed. The unknown journey has allowed me to discover hidden talents and passions that I never would've realized had I earned my degree and began the Hollywood career I coveted for so long. I say to you reading this to JUST KEEP LIVING! Your PIPE Dream doesn't die because your journey takes a detour. You'll gain a wealth of experience that only contributes to your purpose.

I'll leave you with one of my favorite scriptures from Isaiah: "For My thoughts are not your thoughts, Nor are your ways My ways," says the Lord. For as the heavens are higher than the earth, So are My ways higher than your ways, And My thoughts than your thoughts." It's good to know the one in control is always thinking greater of me than I am of myself.

Rewrite History

Remember in the introduction when I asked you to write down your pipe dreams or things you think you'd like to do for the rest of your life and get paid for? Let's revisit those thoughts because this experience may have given you some clarity on what you want to do with the rest of your life. Your list may be identical or have shifted a little bit. Rewrite those pipe dreams. But before you do, I want you to choose a song or playlist that speaks to your soul. Something that gets you centered, focused, and creates a safe space for you.

1. Picture what your life would look like if you were getting paid to do what you love.
2. What industry would you be in?

3. What type of salary or contracts you'd command for your services?
4. What city, state, or even country would you be in?
5. Describe your residence: Condo? Luxury apartment? Duplex? Mansion?
6. What does your love life look like? Are you married, single, or have entanglements?
7. Do you have children?
8. How often do you travel for leisure and or business?
9. What type of impact are you making on your community?
10. What population of people are you helping?

Take your time answering these questions. Free yourself of all expectations placed upon you by family, your culture, society, and your knack for survival. These questions will help you rewrite your pipe dreams, which in turn makes you rewrite your history. Be honest with yourself during this process because you'll then translate this into a vision board. Your P.I.P.E Dream(s) is your birthright. Once you can see it every day, you'll be driven by this internal motivation to live what YOU love! Whether you're a student or a working adult, you have the power to pursue what's been lying dormant in your dreams.

www.ingramcontent.com/pod-product-compliance
Lightning Source LLC
Chambersburg PA
CBHW05165916042
43209CB00004B/962